To B[...] '89
Birthday.
From Graeme

The Little Boy Samuel

by Jane Belk Moncure
illustrated by Paul Karch

THE CHILD'S WORLD
ELGIN, ILLINOIS 60120

Library of Congress Cataloging in Publication Data

Moncure, Jane Belk.
 The little boy Samuel.

 (Bible story books)
 SUMMARY: Retells the Bible story of how the child Samuel opened the doors of the House of the Lord so all kinds of people could come in.
 1. Samuel, judge of Israel—Juvenile literature.
2. Bible. O.T.—Biography—Juvenile literature.
[1. Samuel, judge of Israel. 2. Bible stories—O.T.]
I. Karch, Paul. II. Title. III. Series.
BS580.S2M6   222'.43'0924 [B]   79-12174
ISBN 0-89565-084-3

Distributed by Standard Publishing, 8121 Hamilton Avenue, Cincinnati, Ohio 45231.

© 1979 The Child's World, Inc.
All rights reserved. Printed in U.S.A.

The Little Boy Samuel

The Biblical account of Samuel's childhood is found in *I Samuel,* chapters 1, 2, and 3.

Little Samuel lived
in the House of the Lord.
In the House of the Lord
he lived, long ago,
with Eli, the Priest.

7

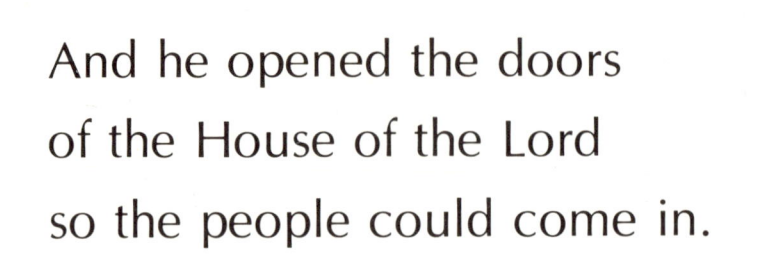

And he opened the doors
of the House of the Lord
so the people could come in.

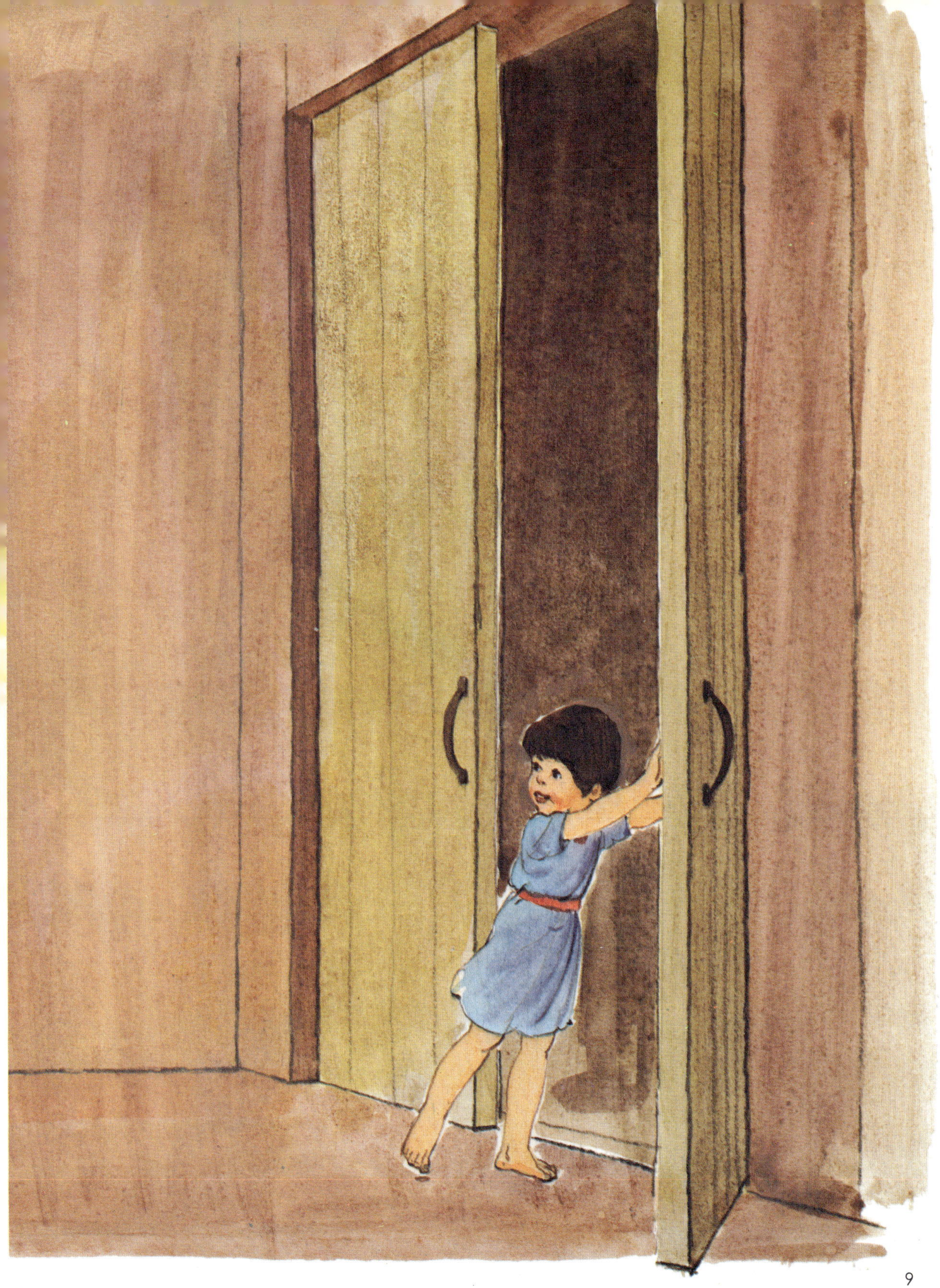

The little boy Samuel
opened the doors
so the shepherds
could come in.

11

They came with their goats
and their dear little lambs.
They came to give thanks
to Jehovah, the Lord—
thanks for their flocks
and their grassy green fields.

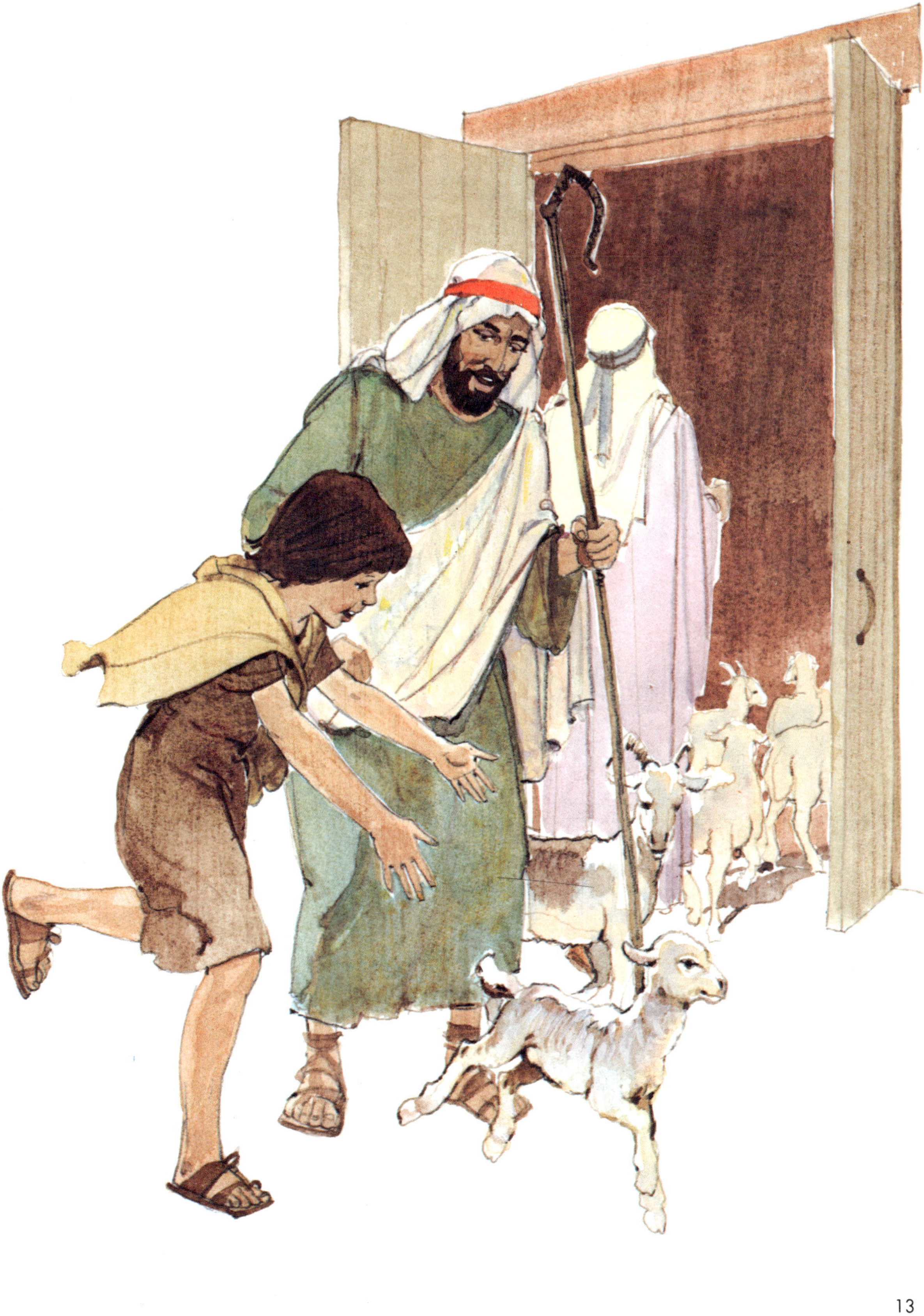

The little boy Samuel
opened the doors
of the House of the Lord,
long ago.
He opened the doors
so the farmers could come
with their figs and olives,
melons and grapes,
and baskets of golden wheat.

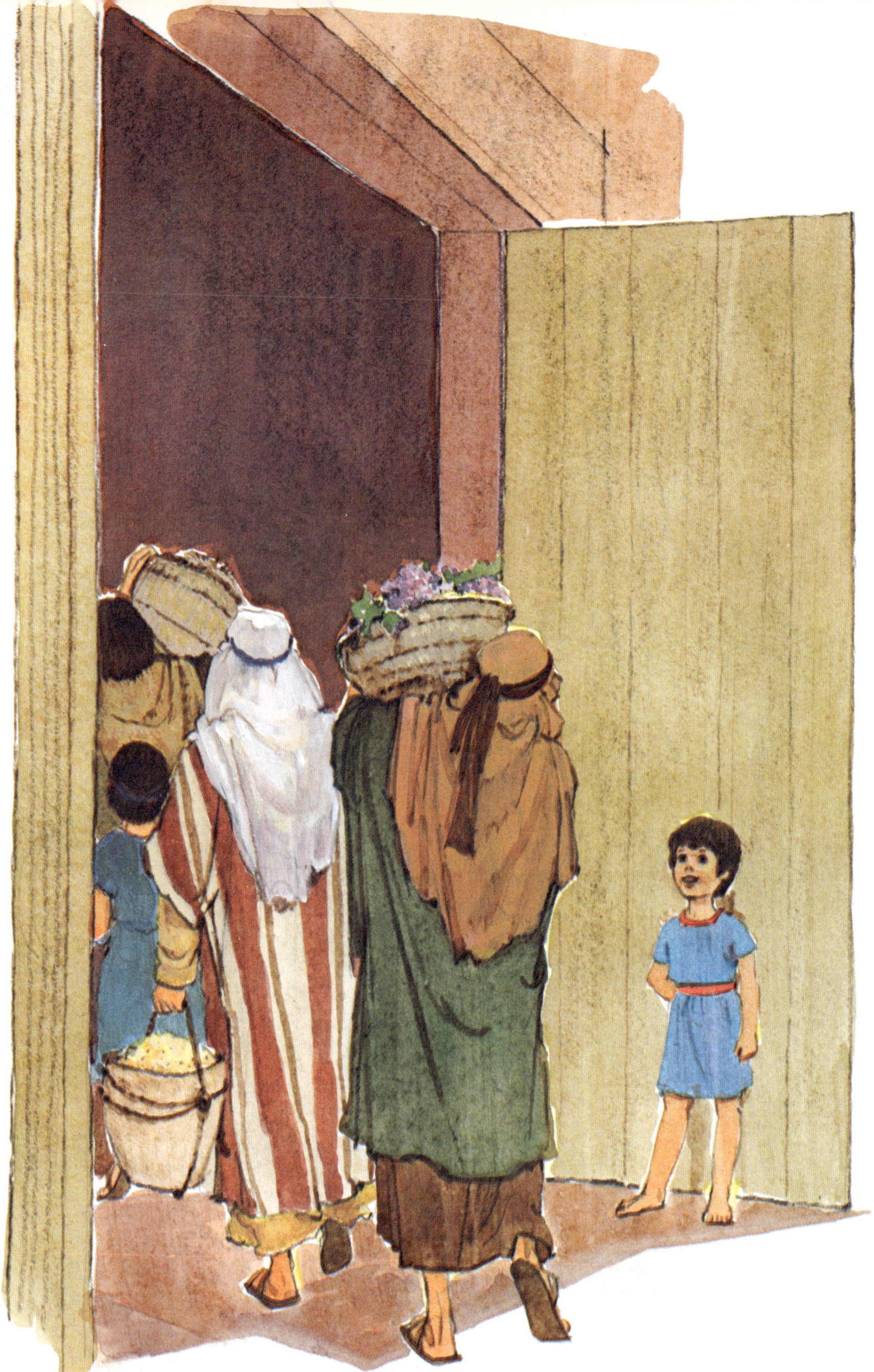

They came to give thanks
to Jehovah, the Lord,
for sending rain
so their crops would grow.
They prayed
a prayer of thanksgiving,
long, long ago.

17

The little boy Samuel
opened the doors
of the House of the Lord
long ago.
He opened the doors
so a sick man could come
and ask God's help
in making him well.

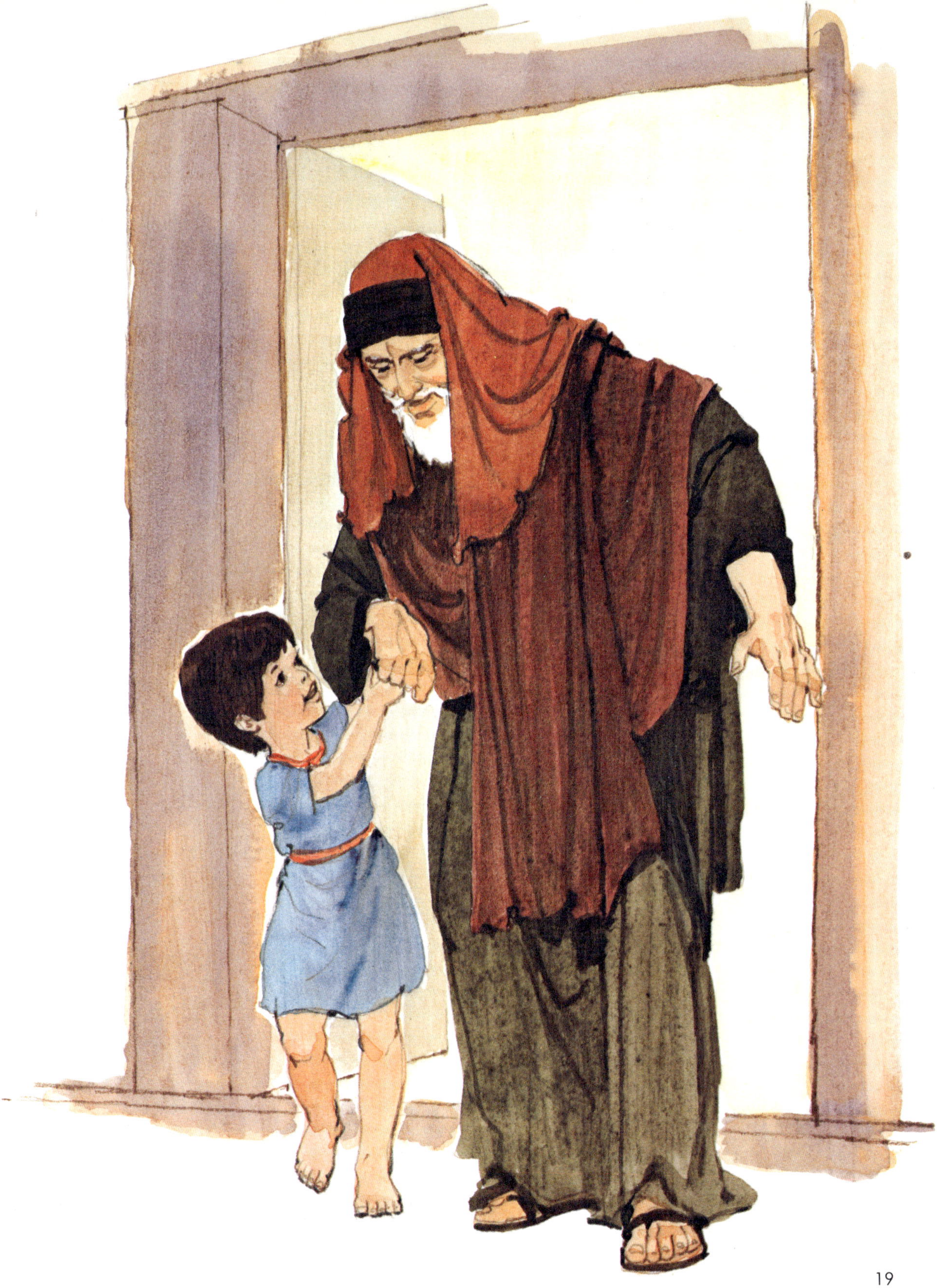

The little boy Samuel
brought a lamp
so the man could see
and gave him water to drink.

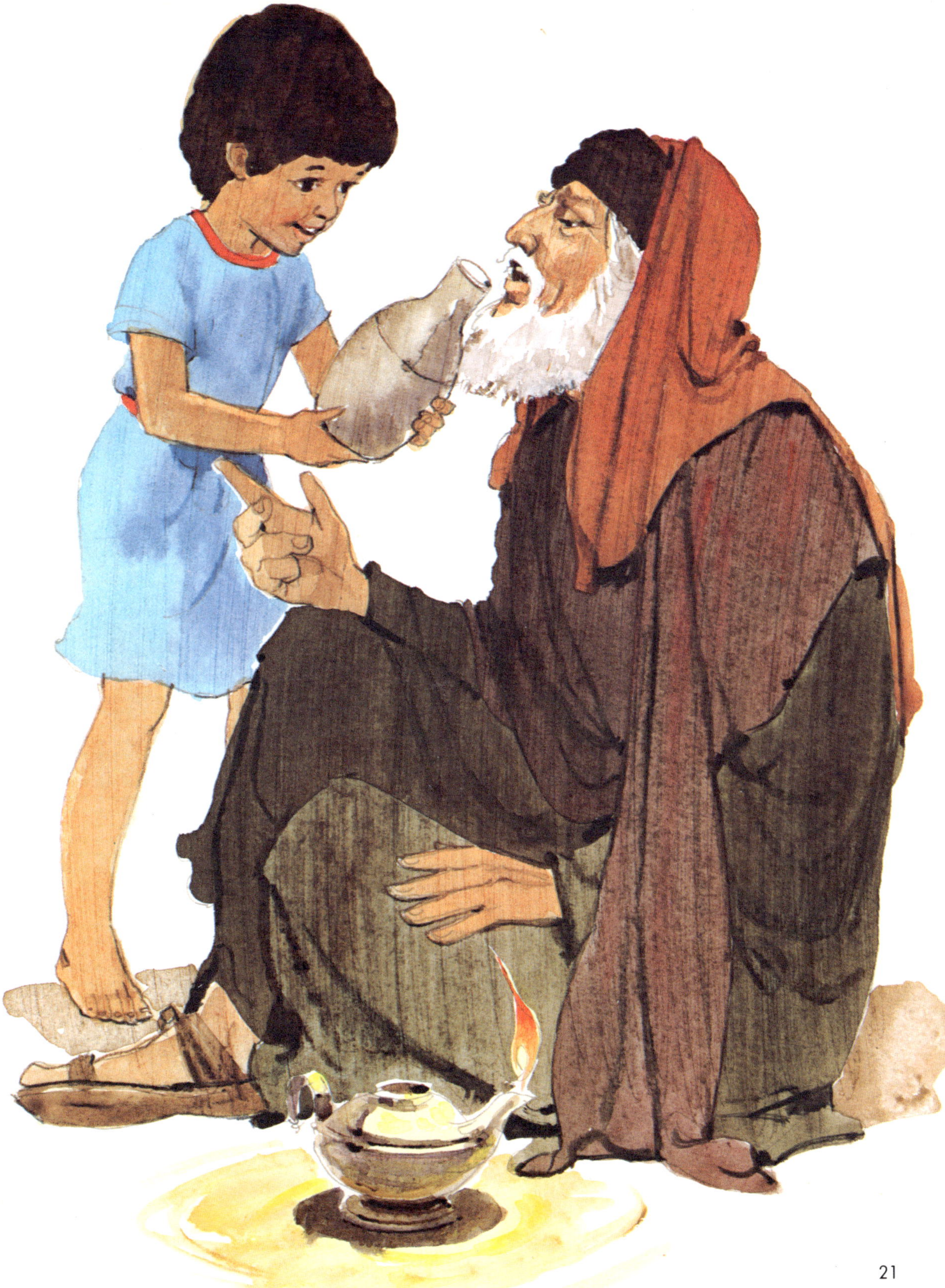

The little boy Samuel
opened the doors
of the House of the Lord
so a blind man
could come in.

23

Samuel led him
by the hand,
for Samuel was a helper
in the House of the Lord,
long, long ago.

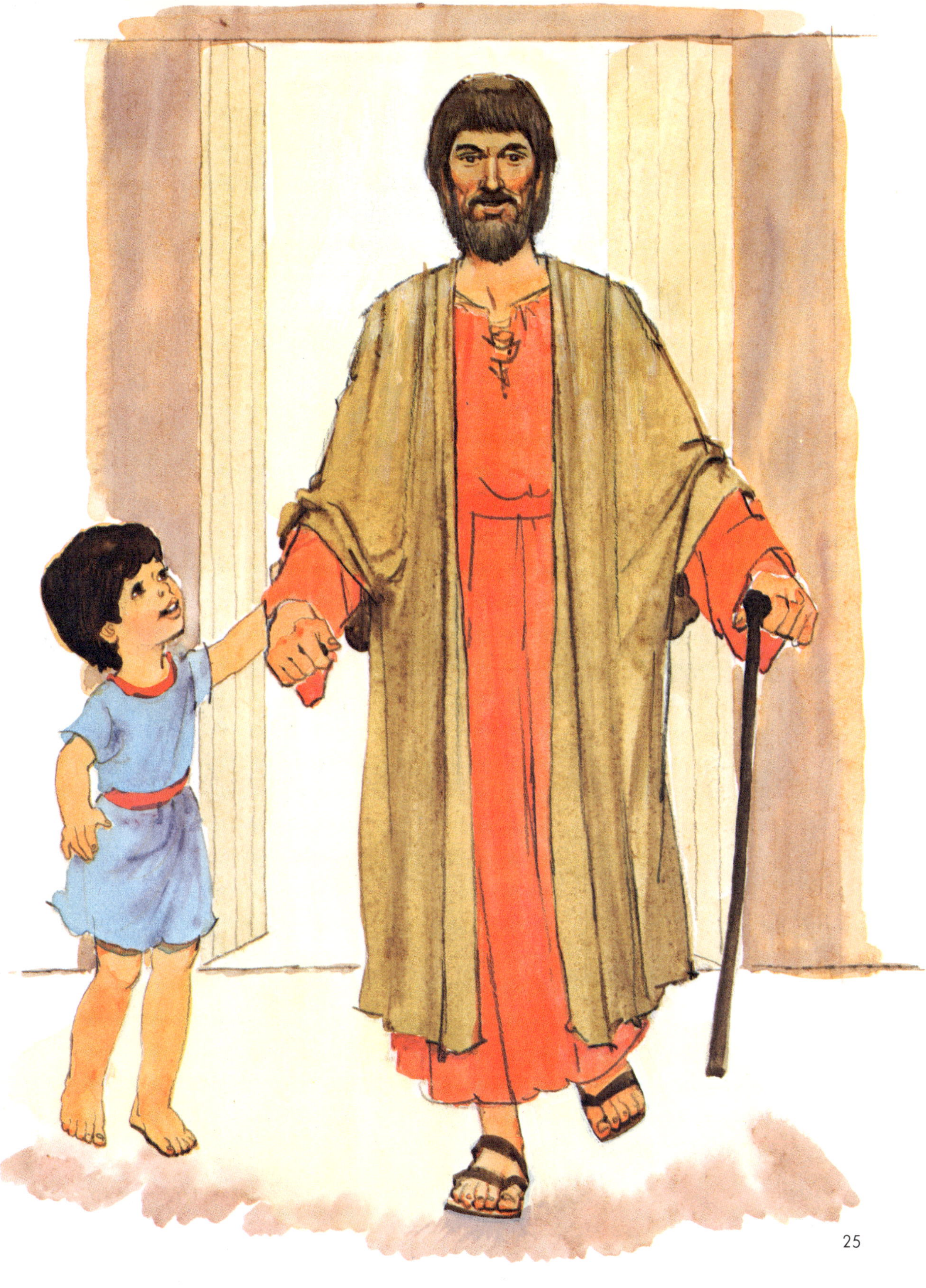

Then the little boy Samuel
opened the doors
of the House of the Lord
so the families could come in.
The fathers, mothers, sisters,
brothers — all could come
into the House of the Lord.

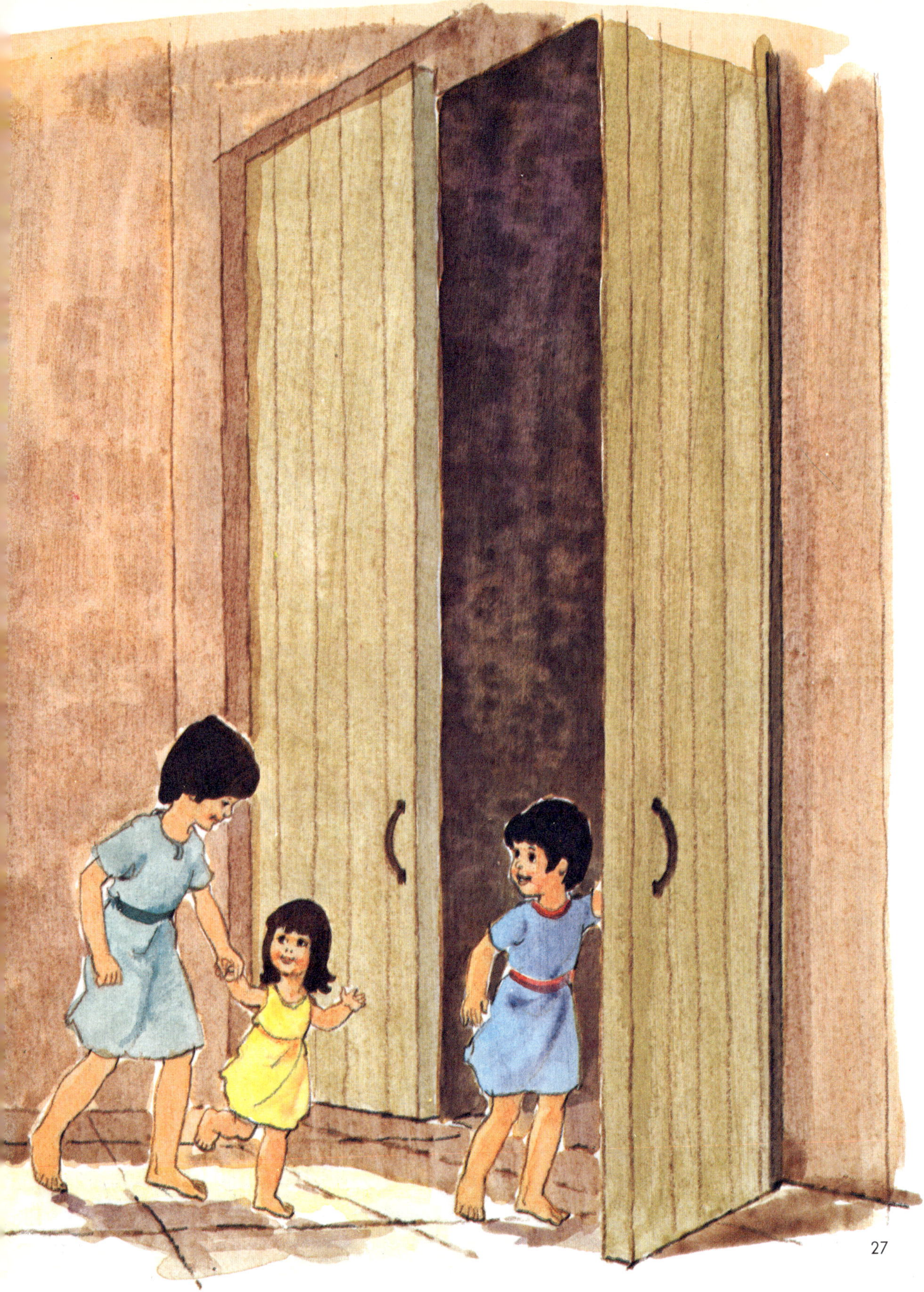

They played the harps and cymbals.
They played the pipes and trumpets.
The little boy Samuel
sang with his friends.

29

They sang a song
to Jehovah, the Lord,
a joyful song
to Jehovah, the Lord.
"Bless His holy name,"
they sang,
long, long ago.

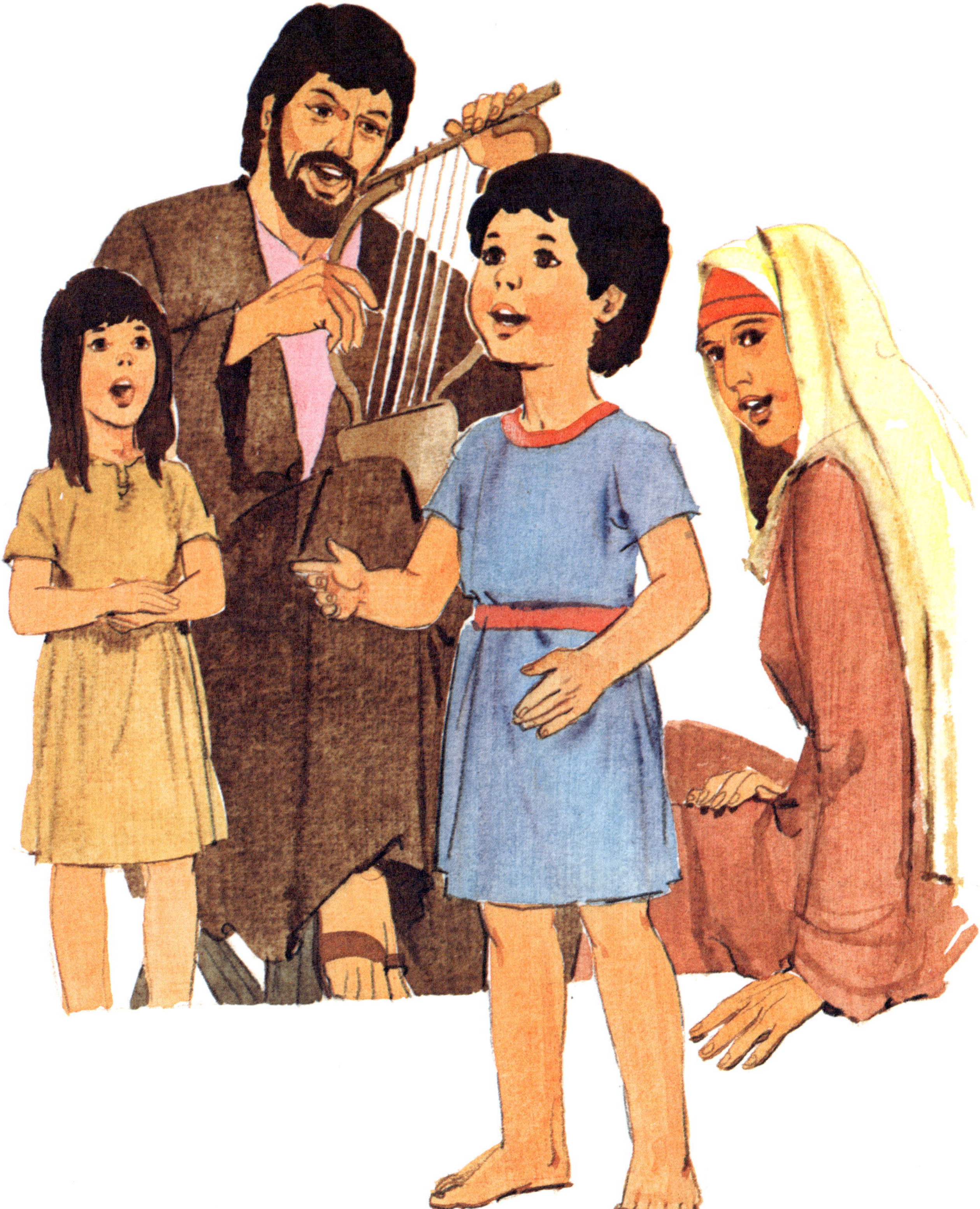

NOTE: Though the Tabernacle was a tent, many authorities believe it became a more permanent structure during the long period it was at Shiloh. *1 Samuel 3:15* does say that Samuel "opened the doors of the house of the Lord."

The Bible does not tell us exactly what Samuel's duties were when he came to live at the Tabernacle, with Eli. But it is reasonable to assume that Samuel might have done all of the things mentioned in this narrative for Samuel "ministered before the Lord." — *1 Samuel 2:18*.